Management 10 x 10

A concise reference of tips, tricks, and guidelines for managers at all levels, in all types of organization

This book is not for dummies! It was written for smart people who want to learn things quickly and easily.

A 10 x 10 Production

First edition July 2010

ISBN: 1453694781

EAN-13: 9781453694787

Acknowledgements

Special thanks to Alec Rowell for editing this book. Alec's advice and suggestions were invaluable. If you find any grammar or spelling errors, please don't blame Alec. I'm sure they were introduced after he completed his final edit pass.

I'd also like to thank my lovely wife Diana for her undying support and encouragement.

Introduction

Effective management is the driving force behind every successful organization. Corporations, government agencies, small businesses, and even non-profits rely on competent managers to achieve their objectives.

Most organizations have an average ratio of one manager for every five individual contributors. Many larger organizations have multi-dimensional hierarchies of management with front-line supervisors managing the people actually doing the work, mid-level managers overseeing the front-line supervisors, and executives directing the activities of mid-level managers. It takes roughly 20% of the workforce to organize the activities of the other 80% and make them more effective and more productive working together as a team.

Most organizations reward good managers. They often receive more compensation, power, status, and prestige as they climb the corporate ladder. However, these privileges usually come at a price. Anyone who has tried it will tell you that balancing the job satisfaction, growth, and development of your employees with the mission of achieving bottom-line results is not as easy as it looks.

Being a great manager is not only difficult; it can be a rapidly moving target. The qualities that some employees value in a manager may be despised by others and a top-notch manager in one organization or situation may fail spectacularly in other, very similar, circumstances. Consequently, there isn't one management style that will work for everyone in every situation. However, there are a lot of fundamental management principles and practices that hold true for top-level, mid-level, and front-line managers, in almost every organization and situation.

Anyone can learn and apply these principles. Management is not a science and it is not an art; it is a craft that can be learned and honed. The only firm prerequisites to being a good manager are compassion, common sense, enthusiasm for accepting the responsibilities of leadership, and the willingness to be accountable for the success or failure of an organization. If you have these qualities, you can learn the skills and gain the experience to be a great manager.

You can spend years learning on the job, reading books, attending conferences, seminars, and workshops (like I did) to acquire an understanding of what it takes to be a great manager or you can get the essence of that knowledge from this book. It presents the basic, universal rules of good management in a "10 X 10" format that is easy to read and comprehend.

This book covers ten essential management concepts and lists the ten most important details successful managers should know to master each of those concepts. It contains a wealth of theoretical information, along with practical guidance and specific ideas that can be applied to real world everyday management situations. This book is an indispensible guide for new managers and a handy reference for more experienced managers.

The Ten Essential Management Concepts

Ten Characteristics of Great Leaders

Effective leaders are at the heart of every successful organization. They provide the vision, guidance, and inspiration their workers need to stay motivated and productive. While all of the leaders in an organization are not necessarily in management roles, great managers are always leaders.

Great leaders:

1. Hire great employees. Hire teams with diverse backgrounds and working styles, avoid only hiring people like themselves, and often hire people better than themselves.

2. Inspire confidence and earn the trust of their employees. Lead by example. Encourage and inspire their teams to reach new heights. Motivate employees through encouragement and positive reinforcement and not through intimidation.

3. Think strategically. Have a clear vision of the future; know where their organization needs to go and how it will get there. Outline a path for others to follow and communicate it clearly and appropriately to the entire organization.

4. Set bold goals. Set goals that are specific, measurable, attainable, relevant, and time-based. Ensure all members of the team understand their roles and responsibilities in achieving the goals.

5. Deflect credit and accept blame.

Are accountable for the actions of their team and take responsibility for mistakes without pointing fingers. Do not hog the limelight when the group is praised.

6. Are honest, sincere, and act with integrity. Are aware of their influence as a role model and realize their decisions and actions define the character and values of their organization.

7. Understand their business. Can analyze complex data and perceive the impact it will have on their organization. Anticipate and recognize problems before they occur and have proven strategies for overcoming them.

8. Know when to cut their losses. Have the courage to admit their mistakes. Base decisions on what is best for the organization moving forward and don't spend time and effort justifying choices they made in the past.

9. Are intelligent, imaginative, and open to new ideas. The only thing constant is change; successful leaders have the foresight to recognize when significant changes around them require changes and are agile enough to adapt to new situations.

10. Always find a way to succeed. Pursue their goals with energy and drive. Consistently push themselves to achieve and won't quit until the task is complete even in the face of adversity.

Ten Core Responsibilities of a Manager

Great managers strive to achieve great results with the resources they have available. They understand that people are their most valuable resource, and they balance the responsibility of efficiently accomplishing the tasks at hand while ensuring their employee's job satisfaction, career growth, and compensation.

Managers are responsible for:

1. Staffing. Recruiting, training, developing, and retaining talented employees is the most important factor in determining whether you will spend the majority of your time and effort babysitting or actually managing.

2. Organizing. Understanding the roles required to efficiently accomplish your objectives as well as the relationships between different groups in an organization is a crucial step in shaping the structure of a successful team.

3. Budgeting. Planning future investments based on expected expenses and revenues requires the insight to understand the benefits of doing something as well as the foresight to anticipate hidden costs and the opportunities lost by doing nothing.

4. Communicating. Being a credible spokesperson capable of disseminating clear and concise information that employees need to do their job effectively inspires confidence throughout an organization.

5. Motivating. Encouraging team members to exceed their individual business and career goals, while working together effectively as a team, helps increase productivity and keeps morale high.

6. Rewarding great performers and dealing with poor performers. Not all rewards are financial. Whether it is done in public or behind closed doors, knowing when to congratulate or chastise a team is an extremely useful motivation strategy.

7. Fostering a safe work environment. Managers set the tone for what is considered acceptable behavior in the workplace. In addition to being a role model, good managers deal with potentially threatening situations and diversity issues immediately and publically.

8. Resolving conflicts. Dealing with differences of opinions and being the final decision maker is one of the most visible tasks managers perform. Resolve disputes at the first appropriate opportunity; they rarely get worked out on their own and tend to fester if they aren't dealt with in a timely way.

9. Monitoring outcomes. Checking results to ensure quality and productivity goals are being met and then using what they learn to improve the process or the product is one task where managers can have the greatest impact.

10. The job satisfaction and career growth of their employees. Understanding what motivates members of your organization, their long and short-term career goals, and helping them achieve those goals is an effective tool managers can use to ensure employees are happy and are striving to excel.

Ten Elements of Strategic Planning

Strategic management is an ongoing process. It is your game plan for defining and refining your organization's core strategies for achieving performance goals. Providing a clearly defined direction and setting priorities energizes an organization and inspires people to work together as a cohesive unit focused on the activities most appropriate for achieving your objectives.

Strategic planning guidelines include:

1. Knowing when to start strategic planning. If your mission statement doesn't reflect current thinking, if you have a tough time setting priorities, or you don't have well-defined objectives, then your organization will benefit from strategic planning. However, you shouldn't go through the process more than once every couple of years unless the business landscape changes drastically.

2. Developing Vision, Mission, and Value Statements. Form a bold vision of where you see your organization in five-to-ten years and clearly spell out long-term objectives and the values that guide your organization.

3. Assessing your current position. You need to know where you are today to clearly understand what needs to be done to achieve your vision. Analyze the internal and external factors that can help you or prevent you from achieving your long range goals. Evaluate strengths, weaknesses, opportunities, and threats.

4. Setting a strategic direction. Convert the mission statement into measurable performance targets. Develop strategies for achieving your long-term goals that leverage your organization's strengths, address weaknesses, exploit opportunities, and minimize threats.

5. Specifying objectives and quantifying results. Establish a timeline for achieving results. Define what you hope to accomplish, who you hope to impact, and how you will define success. Established time-based objectives keep teams from becoming complacent or confused about what they should be doing and when they should do it.

6. Crafting tactics and strategies that achieve results.
A strategy is only as good as the tactics used to execute
it. Develop a specific plan of action that outlines the steps
required to achieve the desired outcomes.

7. Evangelizing the strategic plan. All stakeholders
should understand the overarching principles driving the
organizational priorities that guide their everyday tasks. A
well written plan creates excitement and inspires an
organization.

8. Implementing the strategic plan. Cascade the plan
down organization and ensure it gets used as a guide for
making decisions. Encourage every individual in the
organization to consider whether their everyday activities
are consistent with the objectives in the plan. Use the
plan to guide your day-to-day business decisions; if you
don't use it no one else will feel obligated to.

**9. Reacting to unexpected changes and unforeseen
circumstances.** Great managers often start with a
deliberately planned strategy and hone their plan when
unanticipated situations arise. An organization's
strengths, weaknesses, opportunities, and threats change
over time. No strategy is viable indefinitely and most have
a very short shelf-life. Adapt to the realities of the
situation and refine your plan accordingly.

10. Reviewing the results.

Assess the progress you are making toward achieving
your stated goals and evaluate the outcome. Learn from
your mistakes; use hindsight to set realistic benchmarks
for future strategic plans.

Ten Traits of Highly Productive Employees

Diversity of thought, background, and work style are important to a team; however, great employees all share some common traits, skills, and competencies. Great managers hire based on future potential and not just to fill a position with someone who can do the job today.

Qualities of successful employees include:

1. Intellect. Great employees have the critical thinking skills and intellectual horsepower to learn new skills quickly. They can process complex information, identify key issues, and draw logical conclusions about the impact it will have on the organization.

2. Drive. Great employees strive to achieve results and complete tasks in a timely manner. They seek out new challenges and set lofty goals for themselves and their teams.

3. Self-awareness. Employees must have a desire to improve and a realistic view of their limitations and the contributions they make. The capacity for self-evaluation and the ability to modify their behavior based on feedback is a huge key for employee growth.

4. Accountability. Employees must be trustworthy and responsible. They can be counted on to do what they say when they say they'll do it. They own up to mistakes when they make them and don't blame others for their failures.

5. Enthusiasm. Great employees have a passion for their role and for core organizational goals. They focus on achieving positive results that affect the bottom line. They demonstrate excitement for the work they do and the contributions they make.

6. Creativity. Great employees are inspired, resourceful, and innovative. They are open to new ideas and have the ability to think unconventionally to develop original approaches for solving typical problems or addressing unusual situations.

7. Eloquence. Great employees can articulate their thoughts and get their ideas across effectively and persuasively. They understand how to tailor the language, tone, and timing of a message for the intended audience. They project a positive and professional image of the organization.

8. Esprit de Corps. Great employees are team players. They make others around them better employees. They take pride in the contributions their team makes to the bottom line.

9. Resiliency. Great employees are flexible. They maintain their composure when faced with tough situations. They are energized by change and work effectively in ambiguous or uncertain situations.

10. Confidence. Great employees have the courage to stand firmly behind their convictions and ideas. They demonstrate a strong sense of certainty in their beliefs even when these beliefs are unpopular.

Ten Rules for Evaluating Employee Performance

Formally assessing and rating employee performance and the contributions they make to the overall success of an organization makes them accountable and motivates them to do their best, especially when performance ratings are tied to job security and salary increases.

To evaluate employee performance:

1. Understand the roles and responsibilities of every employee in your organization. Appreciate the skill and expertise your employees need and the amount of effort required to successfully perform their critical job tasks.

2. Set performance standards for each role. Develop an equitable measuring stick for assessing employee performance and the value of their contributions. Your standards must be fair, consistent, and objective.

3. Ensure every employee understands established performance standards. Employees should know the quality and quantity of work they are expected to produce. Employees should also have a clear understanding of which types of behaviors are unacceptable in the workplace.

4. If you have a formal process, keep it simple. Any tools or forms used in a formal evaluation process should be straightforward and unambiguous. The steps in the process and the schedule for completing each step should be clear. Make the review process as easy and quick as possible or you risk loss of productivity and discontented employees.

5. Make employees commit to established goals.

Work with each of your employees to set personal and team objectives that are linked to your organization's key business drivers. The objectives should be specific, hold the employee accountable, and include metrics for determining success or failure.

6. Assess performance on a regular basis.
Performance management should be a year-around process that culminates in a regularly scheduled formal review. Don't wait for an annual review to provide in-the-moment coaching and give your employees feedback on their performance. Nothing in an annual review should be a surprise to you or your employee.

7. Gather relevant feedback.
Solicit feedback for each employee from their co-workers, customers, superiors, and subordinates. The feedback you use to assess performance should come from identifiable sources so that you can take the source into consideration.

8. Deal with poor performers and reward good performers.
Formal performance evaluations are a great opportunity for managers to officially document poor performance; it's the first step toward weeding out employees who can't or won't pull their weight. It is also a great opportunity to re-recruit your top performers by letting them know how much you appreciate their accomplishments and value their contributions.

9. Be as honest and straightforward as possible.
Most performance issues should be dealt with in a face-to-face one-on-one private meeting. Own the message you deliver; after all, it's your assessment. Don't sugarcoat bad news, make excuses, or blame others.

10. Examine performance results holistically.
Look for overall trends year over year and organization-wide. Scrutinize performance assessment results with an eye toward ensuring that all groups are being evaluated fairly and equitably.

Ten Qualities of Successful Mentors

A mentoring partnership is a great way to build your coaching and leadership skills as well as groom the future stars in your organization for success. Additionally, the personal satisfaction you receive from helping others achieve in their careers can often be the most substantial reward.

To get the most from mentoring a protégé:

1. Listen without immediately offering solutions. Start your conversations by putting your protégé at ease. Ask questions or make comments intended to engage and draw them out. Get to the root of issues before you attempt to solve them.

2. Show respect for your protégé's viewpoints. Never be judgmental or condescending and show respect for their point of view even when you disagree. Keep conversations productive and your protégé will feel encouraged to speak openly and honestly about what's on their mind.

3. Empathize. The ability to understand and identify with your protégé's point of view opens doors to the compassion and insight required to be a great mentor.

4. Keep all mentoring conversations confidential. As a mentor, you may be privy to your protégé's personal thoughts and confidential information. Foster an environment where they have the confidence to engage in candid conversations without fear of embarrassment or recriminations.

5. Encourage your protégé to be accountable for their actions. Help them understand the skills and competencies they need to acquire and the factors that may be limiting their growth. Provide them with thoughtful feedback about strategies for addressing their weaknesses as well as ideas for building on their strengths.

6. Set concrete objectives. Help your protégé clarify their life and career goals and examine where they are today. Determine what skills and competencies they need to grow and craft a plan for achieving these goals. Identify distinct milestones that demonstrate real progress toward their objectives and celebrate when important milestones are reached.

7. Be a supporter, advocate, and coach. Always have your protégé's best interest at heart and have a sincere desire to support and nurture their development. Put your own self-interests and the interests of your organization aside even when it may be inconvenient to do so.

8. Do your homework. In addition to sharing your existing knowledge and experiences, take the time to familiarize yourself with the resources available to help your protégé achieve their development and professional goals. Network with business associates inside and outside your organization to look for opportunities to help your protégé to grow.

9. Be a positive role model. How you conduct yourself matters. Always demonstrate high values and principles and conduct yourself with integrity. Be conscious of the example you set for your protégé to emulate.

10. Be a friend. You don't necessarily have to develop a social friendship or spend time with your protégé outside of work. However, forming an emotional bond and developing a sense of caring for your protégé is an essential component of being a great mentor.

Ten Steps for Solving Problems

Managers are frequently faced with complex problems and difficult situations. Great managers evaluate the risks, benefits, and opportunities of any situation, and use this information to craft and implement effective solutions to resolve problems.

To solve problems:

1. Recognize when a decision needs to be made.
Symptoms such as low team morale, sagging profits, or slipping schedules may indicate there is a problem that needs to be addressed. However, keep in mind, some problems don't have a cause and some causes don't have a resolution.

2. Define the problem. Develop an objective problem statement that describes the current situation, explains why it is a problem, how it is happening, and where you want your organization to be once the problem is resolved.

3. Identify the root causes. Research the problem and what led up to it. Separate the causes from the effects and symptoms. Eliminating the root cause of a problem generally leads to a permanent solution, while addressing the symptoms is a temporary fix at best.

4. Take stock of existing resources. Establish the depth of the problem and what resources, such as time, equipment, and people, are available to tackle it. Establish boundaries that limit the scope of solutions to keep your organization from becoming overwhelmed.

5. Identify possible solutions and potential roadblocks. Develop a list of options for solving the problem. Start with obvious solutions but consider all of the alternatives. Brainstorm and encourage the team to come up with creative solutions and contingency plans. Then, create an inventory of obstacles that can limit those solutions.

6. Analyze the alternatives. Weigh the pros and cons of each proposed solution. Perform a cost-benefit analysis to ensure the solution will not be more painful than living with the problem.

7. Select the best solution. Consider all of the facts and figures but rely on your experience, intuition, and judgment to select the solution that you believe has the best chance of solving the problem efficiently and effectively.

8. Socialize the plan. Communicate with all stakeholders to explain the issue, the proposed solution, and how it will affect them. Solicit their feedback and use their ideas and criticisms to improve the plan.

9. Implement the plan. Ensure that everyone in the organization understands their role and the tasks they must perform to implement the solution. Set goals and metrics for success along with a timetable for completion.

10. Evaluate the plan. Use the goals you set to measure the effectiveness of your solution. Does the problem still exist? Was the solution more painful than the problem? Tweak the plan based on what you learned. Reevaluate the results on a periodic basis to make course corrections and develop new processes if needed.

Ten Best Practices for Leading Change

The only constant is change, and with change comes the potential for upsetting the applecart. Fear of the unknown makes people resistant to change, so they often react to it irrationally and unpredictably. However, if managed properly, positive changes for the future can be made without disrupting your organization or lessening short-term productivity.

To effectively lead change:

1. Build your organization's capacity for change.
Teach your management team how and why people react to change and provide them with the support they need to successfully lead change. Dealing effectively with the ambiguities of change is a competency that can be developed in every member of an organization.

2. Identify the need for change.
When the perils of leaping into the unknown outweigh the benefits of averting a crisis or seizing an opportunity, it's time for a change. Understanding the pressures forcing change will help you determine what changes are required and calculate the full cost of implementing change.

3. Analyze the impact changes will have.
Weigh the cost of implementing change against the opportunities lost by doing nothing. Making change for change's sake can be expensive, disruptive, and a major cause of stress in the workplace.

4. Establish specific goals.
Set clear and measurable objectives and develop a timetable for achieving those objectives. People are far more likely to actively participate if they understand what is expected from them and the requirements for achieving a successful outcome.

5. Broadly share your vision for making changes.
Fear of the unknown can sap productivity and be disruptive to a team. Provide as much detail as possible, as early as possible, to avoid misunderstandings. Everyone impacted by the change should understand the rationale behind the change, the schedule for making changes, and what isn't changing.

6. Start by shaking up the status quo. Establish a sense of urgency for making change. To get the ball rolling, it is often necessary to shock people out of complacency and into action.

7. Expect resistance and plan for it. Use objections as an opportunity to deal with negative perceptions. Clear up misconceptions by providing additional information about the benefits of making the changes. The degree to which people resist change is directly correlated to how they perceive the change will impact them.

8. Empower employees to act on the vision. Provide employees with an open path for easily sharing their ideas. Leave room in your change plan to incorporate new ideas into your approach.

9. Make the changes permanent. To prevent your organization from backsliding into old habits reinforce the fact that the change is here to stay. Use every opportunity to point out the correlation between the changes that were implemented and the benefits they have supplied. Ensure the change becomes a part of team culture.

10. Avoid change saturation. The cumulative and collective impact of changes can overwhelm an organization's capacity for change and have negative consequences. Evaluate and manage your "portfolio" of changes to ensure your organization doesn't reach the saturation point.

Ten Strategies for Maintaining Healthy Group Dynamics

People behave differently in groups than they do when they are alone. Informal groups and cliques form a social system in the workplace that influences the interactions among employees. The relationships between people and groups in your organization are dynamic. They can have a positive or negative impact on a team's willingness to learn from each other, to share resources, and most importantly in how they work together across organizational boundaries to achieve common goals.

To maintain healthy group dynamics:

1. Foster a culture that values teamwork. Clearly communicate the expectation that collaboration, cooperation, and accepting input from others are core values of your organization. Look for opportunities to recognize and reward teamwork and collaboration.

2. Be fair. Consider all sides before making a decision. Treat people the way you would expect to be treated and never play favorites. Be transparent in your decision making. Employees may believe they are being treated unfairly if they don't understand the context or reasoning behind your decisions.

3. Set common goals for your organization. Help your employees understand the big picture and the contributions they need to make to help the organization reach its goals. Ensure that all of your employees share the responsibility and rewards for achieving group goals. Groups that share a common fate will naturally pull together and function cohesively as a team.

4. Value diversity. People from different backgrounds and cultures bring different experiences and viewpoints to the table. Respecting individual differences helps with employee morale and productivity, opens opportunities, allows you to recruit the best employees, and decreases the chance of lawsuits.

5. Encourage participation from everyone. Make sure everyone's ideas are heard and given equal consideration. Provide opportunities for every member of your organization to make valuable contributions and to deliver real results.

6. Distribute authority and responsibility. Many mangers make the mistake of trying to do it all themselves. Trust the people working for you to use good judgment and to make wise decisions and then back them up, even if they make mistakes once in a while.

7. Openly reinforce good behavior and discourage bad behavior. Public praise and congratulations provide positive reinforcement. Conversely, if people see a colleague breaking the rules with seemingly no consequences they are likely to start ignoring the rules themselves or become disgruntled.

8. Keep an open door policy. Ensure the lines of communication are kept open up and down the management chain. Every employee should know the process for making complaints or suggestions and feel confident that someone in the chain of command will listen to and address their concerns.

9. Make everyone in the organization accountable. Carve out areas of ownership and responsibility. Each member of your organization should be responsible for the success or failure of the processes, initiatives, and deliverables that are in their control.

10. Develop formal relationship guidelines for your organization. Formalize a set of guiding principles designed to promote trust, dignity, and respect among the members of your organization.

Ten Pitfalls Managers Can Avoid

Managers walk through a minefield of hazards on a daily basis. The decisions they make can have far-reaching professional and legal consequences. Additionally, they can fall into practices that are counterproductive or demoralizing to the organization. Sometimes your legacy as a manager is more about the things you didn't do than the things you did.

To steer clear of hazards:

1. Don't treat employees like widgets. Don't be so focused on the schedule or bottom line that you forget you are managing people. If you treat employees like equipment, you have no right to expect them to be loyal or motivated.

2. Keep it professional. Keep disparaging remarks and personal opinions to yourself and discourage others from gossiping. If you wouldn't want the subject of your conversation to hear what you are saying, you shouldn't be saying it. Avoid embarrassing situations and nurture a culture of openness and honesty in your organization.

3. Don't manage through intimidation. People respond more favorably to requests than orders. Pressure, threats, and intimidation can bring about short-term productivity gains but ultimately they breed resentment and create a hostile work environment.

4. Don't spend all of your time in your office with the door closed. Be open and approachable. Try "Management by Walking Around." Make time to personally observe, coach, and gather feedback from all of your employees. Listening first-hand to their suggestions and complaints is the best way to keep your finger on the pulse of your organization.

5. Don't try to reinvent the wheel. The biggest mistake many new managers make is trying to put their stamp on an organization before they understand all of the intricacies of that organization, its people, and its challenges. Shaking up the status quo isn't always the right approach.

6. Don't try to do everything yourself. Work hard but learn to delegate appropriately. Don't waste time on menial tasks. Focus on inspiring your team to get the work done instead of trying to do it all yourself.

7. Don't bury your head in the sand. Acknowledge and confront difficult, problematic, or uncomfortable situations as quickly as possible. Don't sit around hoping the situation will take care of itself or try to run away from problems believing they might just magically go away. Challenging circumstances provide great coaching opportunities.

8. Don't be the constant cynic. It is good to be skeptical and play the role of devil's advocate once in a while, but perpetually complaining and venting about what's wrong while offering no solutions is a morale killer. Your team will feed off of your attitude so keep it positive.

9. Don't set yourself up to be irreplaceable. From day one you should start grooming potential replacements for every key role in your organization, including your own. Having a solid succession plan with experienced, capable people waiting in the wings ensures your organization will thrive and grow from one generation to the next.

10. Don't be afraid to look stupid occasionally. Check your ego at the door and have the nerve to ask a naïve question or solicit help and advice once in a while. The hallmark of being smart isn't what you know; it's your ability to learn new things.

Authors: If you have an idea for a 10 x 10 book, please send your outline and author bio to:

> 10 x 10 Publishing
> P.O. Box 70033
> Bellevue, WA 98007

Or visit **10X10Publishing.com** for additional information.

Management 10x10

Management 10x10

www.ingramcontent.com/pod-product-compliance
Lightning Source LLC
Chambersburg PA
CBHW051250170526
45165CB00004B/1648